RUIN, BLOSSOM

BY THE SAME AUTHOR

POETRY

The Hoop
Common Knowledge
Feast Days
The Myth of the Twin
Swimming in the Flood
A Normal Skin
The Asylum Dance
The Light Trap
The Good Neighbour
Selected Poems
Gift Songs
The Hunt in the Forest
Black Cat Bone
All One Breath
Still Life with Feeding Snake
Learning to Sleep

FICTION

The Dumb House
The Mercy Boys
Burning Elvis
The Locust Room
Living Nowhere
The Devil's Footprints
Glister
A Summer of Drowning
Something Like Happy
Ashland & Vine

NON-FICTION

A Lie About My Father
Waking Up in Toytown
I Put a Spell on You
The Music of Time: Poetry in the Twentieth Century
Aurochs and Auks

RUIN, BLOSSOM

John Burnside

CAPE POETRY

1 3 5 7 9 10 8 6 4 2

Jonathan Cape is part of the Penguin Random House group of companies
whose addresses can be found at global.penguinrandomhouse.com

First published in the United Kingdom by Jonathan Cape in 2024

penguin.co.uk/vintage

A CIP catalogue record for this book is available from the British Library

ISBN 9781529909258 (Trade paperback)

Typeset in 11/13pt Bembo Book MT Pro by Jouve (UK), Milton Keynes
Printed and bound in Great Britain by TJ Books Ltd, Padstow, Cornwall

The authorised representative in the EEA is Penguin Random House Ireland,
Morrison Chambers, 32 Nassau Street, Dublin D02 YH68

Penguin Random House is committed to a sustainable future
for our business, our readers and our planet. This book is made
from Forest Stewardship Council® certified paper.

In memory of my sister,
Elaine McVeigh

neues Leben blüht aus den Ruinen

Schiller

CONTENTS

APOSTASY

ASYLUM

BLOSSOM

APOSTASY

A FOOTNOTE TO COLOSSIANS

For ye are dead, and your life is hid
Colossians 3:3

Let us remember
the stillborn: how they

cede their places here
with such good grace

that no one ever
speaks of them

again.
In school,

we placed them, carefully,
in Limbo,

deep in the folds of smoke
and snowfall, where

their names would never
find them:

pagan, now,
and immaterial,

like phantoms,
or that

boy I sometimes saw
in polaroids,

the one they said
was me.

NATIVITY

A spill of yew
like Christ's blood
in the snow;
and somewhere in the hedge,
just yards away,
a fleck of presence
waiting to be born.

No angel at the gate.
No guiding star.
We make this world
from gravity and light
and we alone, God's grace
by other means:

a flock of redwings
flitting through the fog,
woodrush
and fescue,
wintergreen,
Rose of Sharon.

MIDNIGHT MASS

We brought the starlight in
fresh from the cold,

a rumour on the skin
of some old

fiefdom, pagan, kindred to the other
animals – *the boarhound and the boar*,

the gaunt deer on the roads
like refugees.

Convinced of nothing,
least of all the saints,

I spent my last prayer
on a plaster

Virgin, paintwork
flaking on an upraised

finger, seams
of gypsum

in the creases
of her veil,

but nothing came to pass,
beyond the scent

of spruce and tallow,
menthol, *L'air du temps*,

and later, when we walked home
after Mass,

I asked the sky for nothing
but the blue

of daybreak, first sun,
magpies in the snow.

VERSES FOR A SAMPLER

Rain at the gates
and the ghost of a mother is here.
Pink-lipped with the blush
of Candlemas, and plainly
fabled, she is older than the girl
who raised us, less
impersonal, though
not above suspicion.

Nightly we lay her down
in her bed of needles,
patient as mice, enthralled
by the thought
of Forever;
nightly we wait in vain
for the *Ecce Virgo*,

a local hajj, the spell
of alpenglow,
a phantom horseman
from some Medieval
woodcut, *Homo*
ludens, with a taste for calculus.

Thou knowest, Lord,
the secrets of our hearts:
a sea-wind blowing in
from street to street.

A final orchard.

Blossom in the ruins.

OUT-TAKE FROM THE GOSPEL OF NARCISSUS

Another skin has come
to nothing, like the snow that fell all day

and melted
in the space between the trees.

Another shadow, cousin to the one
I wanted, when I came in from the cold,

an old Believer, skilled
in saddle-stitch

and lorinery, my elders
gathered round the bonfire with their dogs

and shotguns, patient, ready to begin,
and every man alone beneath the stars.

SKETCH FOR A STABAT MATER

Two, two, the lily-white boys,
Clothed all in green

As if there was a Queen, or miles
of starlight in the backroom where I played
the shadow of a lily-white
in aspic,

I kept faith with the gravity
of objects
and waited for the carriage to arrive
that someone from the past would surely send

to fetch me, horses
lifelike in the dark,
a murmur in the hall that might have been
a spring rain, or a dawning, all I knew

from Old Moore and The Joyful Mysteries
come good at last, as if my heart was true.

THE HERESY OF THE FREE SPIRIT

Visible only in rain, or the blue of daybreak,
more of a thought than a form I could have named,
heaven was void
and the angels were always too bright
to be observed.

No God to speak of there, beyond the glide
of something at the far end of the yard
that never came to pass,
though it was true:

a hunger, pure and simple, like the nub
of pulse and slime
that would have made a soul
had I been born with nothing to repent,
and nothing to forgive, save grace and favour.

CONCERNING GUILE

Because I have mislaid the hush
of boyhood (snowfalls;

shadows in the trees)
too often I have been

indelicate.

And yet, beyond the provinces
of guile, there is

an *autremonde* more
Tir na Nog than

not,
        though not
the refuge I had wished for,

being lost.

If this skin shows too much, let it be
flayed: not

sweetly, but with no great
drama, ice

or laser in the lull
of witching-hour.

No afterlife to come, nor any
persons who aspire

to martyry, dismantled as they are
by Being

Beauteous
                    which is no life at all.

SWEET JAMS AND SPIKENARD

And they understood none of these things:
and this saying was hid from them, neither
knew they the things which were spoken.
Luke 18:34

A skinned child
in the field, just raw enough
to be immaculate,
I hoped I would not fall
to wedlock,
or the snare
of Mother Church.

No summers, then,
that I remember now,
no afterburn
of neon on my tongue,
only the grace
to nurse a false amen
through parlour games
and Quinquagesima.

That Covenant
is lost, Gethsemane
gone down to dust
and buried in the stone,
and nothing in this house
that I can use,
no alibi for love, no *comme il faut*,
no motion in the heart
that is not blood.

AUTO-DA-FÉ

Unshriven, and impervious to doubt,
he's out there, with his Doppelgänger smile,

shining a light through the Tree
of Knowledge, almost

saintly in his armature
of fire.

One of the chosen, practised in the art
of touch-me-not, he constantly arrives

at weightlessness, a wick of skin and bone
too lifelike to be true;
                                        and yet he goes

unquenched, a beacon
blazing in the sun,

my sinless other, bending
to the flame,

so pure and bright,
he almost pulls me in.

ASH WEDNESDAY

Abandon was its own
safe haven, one more incidence
of comfort, cindered palms
and chrism in the likeness
of a cross
– pulvis es, et in pulverem reverteris –

a loose stitch in the heart
made visible: my mind
a flashlight ghosting the walls
at change of shift,
my body hand-me-down
and fictive, almost
Lenten, cleansed
and whittled: nerveless, hollow to the bone

– et mittere digneris sanctum Angelum tuum de caelis,
qui benedicat, et sanctificet hos cineras –

LITHA

In summer, it was harder to be churched;
the pagan gods were out, their sentries
drifting through the sunlit

chapel, pollen
scattered on the flagstones like some timeless
scripture from a world before the Word.

Set loose from school,
I wandered with the bees
through Willowherb and Himalayan

Balsam
        catching
shadows in the shadows: inklings, figments of the land's
imagining;

and nothing to reveal, beyond the hum
of incarnation:
sun on the backlot, mayweed, that clinging smell

of bird rot in the grass, like
angel spoor. How sweetness is always
ruin. No

Hereafter. Always now.

A NOTE ON THE SETHIAN HERESY

For lust of knowing what should not be known,
We take the Golden Road to Samarkand.

James Elroy Flecker

A shred of Samarkand, but not
begotten, like the navy-drab
of worship.
                    No more
chapel, no more
sinner at the gate,

though shadows pass, gigantic on the sand,
and softly through the silence
beat the bells.

I thought it might approximate
to home, so very

picturesque
and measured,

like a service
of remembrance:

fragments of *très riches heures*,
scenes from a masque,

a stronghold sure
                              against the years
of loss.

APOSTASY

Search me, O God, and know my heart:
try me, and know my thoughts
Psalms 139:23

At one time,
when there might have been a God,
the side-streets vaguely
convent, gospel
whispered down the galleries
of rain,

I would have been awake for almost
nothing in the perishable world,
the Presence half-revealed, improbable,
lighting the hedge like a flame
in the green
of morning.

No convent now.
Only the sway of matter and a hint
of distance, almost
perfect, like a favourable *feng shui*,
or like the sudden lull that comes
late in the afternoon,
when an angel passes:

sunlight dusting the pines
by the harbour wall
and nobody saying a word
till day is done,
pilgrim again, beyond all destination,
white in the light of the moon, white in the dawn,
white in the daylight
and haunted by nothing at all.

CHURCH

We thought there must be something
still to come,

a presence in the garden that had waited
years to be revealed, the way

the clock-tower in a snow globe
waits for snow.

Easter again. The streets are paved
with blossom in this tiny Germantown

of *Ordnung* and regret that we mistake
so readily for home (since home exists):

the church, the steeple, windows barred with gold,
an erstwhile god implicit in each stone.

ASYLUM

FLOWERING CURRANTS

I would step through that scent on the way
to nowhere, adder's tooth
and cullet in the grass, my body
suddenly akin
to April rain;

chancing my luck, at large in the noonday sun,
I crossed into the shadows, where a boy
could sing himself to sleep and wake up
naked and abandoned, scarred with touch

and full of voices that were not his own,
his mouth a bruise, all memory a blur,
and everything he knew of House and Home
abandoned to the greenwood
like a snare.

HYMN TO THE SUBJUNCTIVE

Even when nothing is there, it still occurs:
like a bird I recall from childhood, maybe a wren,
or a sedge warbler perched on a reed
at the edge of the meadows.
Close to invisible now, my shadow wakes
to juniper and new snow in an empty
garden, fox-prints
trailing off to what might be
infinity, across a blank of lawn:
and there I am, or would be, if I were,
a lost boy, raised on figs and simnel cake,
bright as a penny, perfect in Latin grammar,
the one who lived to tell another tale,
true at last, like rain, or hieroglyphics.

A REPLY TO WALLACE STEVENS, WITH A LINE FROM JOHN DONNE

Cold in the shade, and yet, by afternoon
the snow is burning off along
the fence-line, where it lay in drifts for weeks,
a chill white, warming slowly to a blur
of slush and haze.
                                I don't have a mind

of winter. Only the timeworn saltlick of a heart
which can by no way be express'd
but negatives,
                        but nothing is more erotic than the way
the snowmelt spills and spends into the ditch,
still cold as ice, but mesmerized with green,

and though there's nothing here that I could name,
I feel it, Mesozoic, intimate,
a changeling on the cusp of something else,
not one thing or the other: something else.

BEDLAM VARIATIONS

While we look not at the things which are seen,
but at the things which are not seen: for the things
which are seen are temporal; but the things which
are not seen are eternal.

2 Corinthians 4:18

I

How will the posthumous survive, without
the memory of heaven we devise
from field guides and the Book of Common Prayer?
We are not real, though everyone is true
to something, be it
Bedlam, or the customs that pertain
to cutting tools, or Christian martyry;
a random staircase miles deep in the woods;
a clown face in the dark; another dawn.
At noon, the cats go hunting in the park,
a fitful Angelus of shrieks and whines:
pinpoints of blood in the gravel, clutches of fur,
that absence, like a sinkhole in the light,
where anything might fail: a bird, a star.

II

Summer in Bedlam. Summer along the coast.
Lilac and Philadelphus in the thin
sweet haze around the gates to the Botanics.
Nostalgia for the earth, the perfumed shade
of woodruff and Solomon's seal; an old
nostalgia for the creatures in their world:
things seen, as I am seen, and things unseen,
absolved of what I once mistook for rapture.
Alone on the ward, I leave the windows
open, so the bees can come and go,
and turn back to my *Boy's Own Book of Birds*,
saying the names aloud, to keep them true,
till, word by word, with ruin in my head,
I fold into the light, and I am blossom.

III

Are you certain it's the nurse who sings
so sweetly, when the corridor goes dark,
and something from the far side of the grounds
comes stealing in to flutter at the glass,
a lilting song that seeps into the room
from just beyond, all hesitance and longing?
It might be her, but there's a chance it's not,
the sound is so unlikely, and the voice
like nothing I have ever heard before,
a creature thing, more plaintive than the wind
that skitters down the back stairs in
the small hours, when the visitors are gone,
a slowed moan through the walls, too sweet to bear,
first here, then there, and nowhere to be found.

IV

I said, 'Is it good, friend?'
'It is bitter – bitter,' he answered

Stephen Crane

No one would hear us now,
if we chose to speak,
not even the dead; and the angels
have yet to appear.
Yet something is with us, here,
in the blue of dawn,
a face between dog and wolf
on the day-room wall;
and, beige by design, we inherit the sins
of the mother:
the taint of love, like venom in a jar
of honey, good, but bitter, always
bitter, like forgiveness for the sin
of being, but not being what was asked.

V

This afternoon goes back to Nineteen
Forty, milky tea with Empire
biscuits, and the dayroom wireless set
to THIRD or is it HOME? I'm
swaddled in the beauty of Largactil,
waiting for Mrs Miniver to step
so lightly through the door that no-one else
will notice, floribunda
roses from her garden and a box
of homemade apple cake, or *langues de chat*,
come from the world that continues in
my absence: births and marriages and all the recent
posthumous, departing on the wind
through halcyon, or sleep, to who knows where.

VI

Walk to the edge of the grounds.
Look to the south.
The town is lit too soon, from street to street,
empires of light against the coming dark.
No streetlights here. We drift into the grey
of evening, while the trolley makes its rounds,
bringing the sweet hiatus of Largactil,
a local empery of Chinese
lanterns, shadows, some of them our own.
A Hazel Moon, the other animals.
We hear them moving closer in the dark,
all glide and whisper, glances, shadowings;
they call us to themselves, we sing them home:
a kindred we had never hoped to find.

VII

Oh! nos os sont revêtus d'un nouveau corps amoureux.
Arthur Rimbaud

In Bedlam house, there is no remedy
but halcyon, a Silk Road in the mind
lit with a thousand lanterns; minarets
and hanging gardens; strongrooms piled with jade
and lapis; safflower; crates of *blanc de chine*.
Summer again: the finches come and go,
as if there was an otherwise we all
could navigate, with nothing but the light
to guide us, siskin green
and umber, cherry red, the many whites
of service-tree and cirrus, all those
presences we never thought to find,
but follow, till we see ourselves writ whole:
new bodies, clothed with amorous new skins.

VIII

Before the fall, the woods were full of clues,
but no one saw the beauty of the serpent,
only the dew trails winding through the grass
where god had been, before he came to naught.

No gods in Bedlam: angels on the ward
at daybreak, martyrs laid to rest
in coverlets of blood, a play
of shadows in the cold refectory,

but all our gods have vanished from this house,
disheartened by the beauty of a world
they made, but could not govern.

Terror by night; the arrow that flieth by day;
and yet we live, attentive to the light,
eyes at the treeline, new shapes crossing the lawn.

IX

If need be, I could live on carrion.
Quiet now, and more inclined
to hunker in and listen, clicks
and whistles through the trees, but nothing
visible, or nothing I could name.
Strange, how the moment
fails to go on for ever;
and yet the dead return, on days like these,
awkward and deferential, loth to speak,
knowing that we now know what they knew
and chose not to disclose, for pity's sake.
In turn, we pity them: their chronic hurt,
the things they bartered for, and could not use,
the price they paid to say: *we are not lost.*

X

If they return, the posthumous will be
as tender as a bruise, run under icy
water, unencumbered by the weight
of seasons no one else
has witnessed, something animal behind
each gesture, though I thought they would have paled
to nothing, having learned
to hold their peace.
I say this for the sake of those
who still remain, the quick, the not yet born,
the suddenly discarnate, come to light
as glitches in the fabric, all
the shadows in a looking glass that seem
familiar: seen things, forged from things not seen.

THE ANATOMY LESSON OF DR WILLEM VAN DER MEER

after Michiel van Miereveld

No one believes in heaven any more,
only the burden of air, forced from the lungs,
equivalent in weight to certain
songbirds, say a bullfinch, or a thrush.

Too small, and oddly
formal, white as frost,
the corpse lies gaping on a wooden board,
a stillness that no calculus could measure;

and, foreign to the light, as if
contrived of rope and wax,
the meshwork of the innards is laid bare
to let whatever spirit they might hold

unravel from the flesh
and bleed away.
Someone has covered the face
with a scrap of gauze.

Beyond the window,
in the smoke and gold
of Hallowmas, the living go unmasked
from house to house, their faces painted on

in likenesses of what they love or fear
when night comes: ghosts
suspended in mid-air,
the feel of someone watching: no one there.

PRAYER

Deliver me from nothing, save the thrill
of perish; place my next breath on the scales
as counterweight to all I know of guile.
Let nothing be so precious as to
linger through a night of summer rain,
when everything is cleansed: the heart, the tongue,
the love of ruins, kinship, wildering;
and let me not forget the scintillance
of new snow in the trees
by Brewster's Yard,
beech mast on the farm roads
flecked with ice, that constant
singing in the fence wire, like the hum
that lingers on, when storyline is done.
Shelter me now, but send me on my way
at daybreak, when the town I could have loved
is locked in sleep, too perfect to recall:
shuttered kiosks, windows bleared with dew,
house martins threading the streets
in the fretwork of dawn.

AT THE COMMUNITY POOL

What if the one who tracks me, stroke for stroke,
is more than just my shadow on the tiles?

Another swimmer, gliding through the sun-starred
water, some new frequency

my skin has yet to learn,
as if the pool was stranger than the field

of glints and echoes
I was schooled to find,

and more than I imagined: not the false
prerogative of others, only

water, sky, my echo calling home
from somewhere in the deep end, right as rain.

BLOSSOM

AUBADE (IN MEMORIAM J.P.)

Morning in lockdown. Shadows in the yard,
Quink-blue and gradually
shifting, like those eels we used to see
above the weir, thick
whipcords of lust
and instinct, surging
headlong through the mystery of grass.
Forty years on, but all I have to do
is close my eyes to see her
cycling to Cherry Hinton in that dust-grey
skirt she used to wear, the dawn light
following the river back to town
– and every summer
proximate, since then, though she was gone
before the mist set in
and anyway, it wasn't what we thought:
the true romance
was place, the faint
continuum of rain on Byron's Pool, the passing
moment, when an owl skimmed overhead
and left me here, years
later, half a mile
of Buddleia and birdsong to the nearest
traffic, threads
of damp along the walls,
but warmer than the house I thought
would shield me: first sun
streaming through the trees,
no I, no us, but just beyond the fence,
a skylark in the near field, flush with song.

SKETCH FOR A TATTOO

Imagine she was still
The Girl, her voice
like tinsel on the air, her hair
like rain,

I would not woo her now,
schooled as I am
in quarantine, the minor
mysteries behind me, braille for skin,

and all my former lives
prêt-à-porter,
The Ace of Cups, The Mask,
The Hierophant,

the Lost Boy in the washroom
flensed and dried,
his salt hide inked with hearts
and mother love.

MAN AND WIFE

On days like these,
her sorrows seem
elective: purest
gesture, like the fur trim on a stole
the queen wears
for her sister's execution;
while somewhere
in the backrooms of the year,
the Cathar in him
dreams in honeydew
of how things might have been
had they been saved:
an Afterwards
implicit in the light,
no shadows anywhere,
besides their own.

TO THE FORMER BRIDE

Resume the veil, close
cousin to the stain
of no one's kiss;

go walking
in the garden; watch
for thorns;

pretend you know
how best to count
your blessings

and leave me
to the hush
of Afterwards.

I like it better here,
beyond the pain
we practised then,

you in your marbled
parlour, almost
spinstered,

though the bed still had the feel
of silk to it:
a sleekness like the end

of sisterhood
or what your mother took
for breach of promise,

glad you were betrayed
as she was, all that
honeymoon and guile

folded and put away
in bags
of lavender and frost, your future

patient to the end
and allied to the Rose-Red
blemish

in each crease of every dress
you wore for their sake,
happy to show willing.

ACQUIRED MEMORIES OF AUTUMN COLOUR

Of Tupelo, I know enough to wish
for nothing, save the gist
of a Hereafter,

a slow dissolve to somewhere less
elaborate than this, but still
unfinished, like the dream that carries on

without us, frost
and lamplight in the dark
interior, a distance so exact

that nobody could ever choose
to leave it for the minor *Reich*
of home.

For years we lived like actors in a silent
movie, lit too well
and haunted by the lines we could not say,

convinced that someone there was not
accounted for, a sweetness on the wind
that might just turn

angelic, one last drift of so-to-speak
that seemed unlike,
though much of it was gold.

BROTHER

How dead he was, and yet I took him home
in spirit, punctual
as Candlemas and cousined to the moon

as I was not, part
cuckoo-bird, part
Holy Innocent.

At Whitsun and Immaculate Conception,
I fattened him on wisps of monochrome,
a panoramic view of old

Vienna, child
inventories of crystalware and grain;
and so we lived, apocryphal and slight,

a false Byzantium of salt and stars,
no lanternlight, beyond what came to hand:
The Book of Deer, *The Idylls of the King*.

AFTER SENECA

quos amor verus tenuit, tenebit
Seneca the Younger

The heart is not intact.
It never was.

It founders
in the provinces

of Thou, a ransacked
treasury of Lost

and Found, an ancient
bonfire in the gap between

two borders, windfall
plums and month-long

snowdrifts in the schoolyard, where
not You nor I remains

to listen,
till the sway of what is heard

unspools by slow degrees
from what is not.

POEM ON A LINE BY ADAM ZAGAJEWSKI

just and unattainable, unattainable and splendid
Adam Zagajewski

Strayed from the angels, blind
to the minor saints,
the only vow we keep
is quarantine;
that promise to be ahistorical
and, so, as nearly
perfect as the days
allow.
The house is full
of still-lifes
everything
suspended in a light that never
ceases to be final
apples
paling in a wicker
basket, Cézannesque
and bruised
to sepia
a spill
of almonds
in a cracked Imari bowl,
so still, we think
of how it must have been
in childhood, when the dead
would come to call,
familiar spirits, pink
and litmus blue,
arriving
from the hinterland of rain.

Memory
fails: days
lengthen into weeks,
then months;
no history to tell
                    or nothing much
beyond a casual sense
of interregnum:
porch-lamps giving way
to daylight in an empty
courtyard
            traffic up and down
the High Street
                  boys
in butcher's bibs
                    a liveried parade
of buses from the depot to the furthest
outskirts, mostly
empty now, but
lit against the grey
of just-past-dawn.

Summer is done
                    and yet
the world goes on
arriving at itself
for no known
reason: just
and unattainable.
No reason
for the wind along
the coast road, scrawling
ciphers in the sand,
no reason
for a parliament of rooks

to gather at the far end of our yard,
havering back and forth between a stand
of beech trees
and some kingdom close at hand
known only to themselves

– and no good

reason to be here
at all

other than here

as such

where all we know

is weather
and the slow purl of the heart

itinerant

but touched
with splendour:

on the cusp

of homelessness

yet

pilgrim

finding

refuge where we least
expect it:
autumn;

sunlight on the bay;

the usual data:

distance;

movement;

stars.

IN MEMORIAM

I knew one thing: night too needed no explanation

Adam Zagajewski

He missed the spring:
a slow pour through the eaves,
snowmelt flooding the streets, the gutters singing.
Aconites bloomed in the last
pockets of grit and ice
by the old canal,
deer mapped the fence-lines, honeybees
quartered the yards.

No reason, now, to talk about the dead;
I turn a corner and the wind gusts in
from everywhere, its salt touch on my lips
a fragment from the Book of Genesis;
and everything comes clear, no explanation:
even in lockdown, the mixed scent of sugar and ozone,
sun on the courthouse, plum blossom ghosting the square.

WULF-MONATH

A wintering;
                              and everything we know
is hearsay: ravens

picking at a blood-knot in the snow, the village
lost, two miles away, the roads

impassable.
      All summer,
there were others in the house

disguised as children, charmless, ravening,
but clothed, as children are,

in swansdown, proofed
like saints against the day

of judgment, when the livestock in the barn
grow weary of themselves, their textbook forms

reduced to hoof and bone, their dream of light
discarded for this banquetry of slops

on which we feed,
though no-one here is lean.

WINTER SUTRA

What I miss about the old house is the way
we lived alone on certain afternoons,

in spite of memory
and common prayer;

a stillness at the far end of the lane
where anything might happen for as long

as nothing did; the stopped clock in the hall;
the frequency of something yet to come

but quietly deferred: a local
exercise in grace or anamnesis.

Windfall plums. A vase of feather-grass.
The lives of others. New rain at the fenceline.

A BRIEF NOTE ON THE INTERREGNUM

There were so many fathers then,
boot-prints running out into the snow
and never coming home, the hum
of elsewhere, every time we stopped
to listen. Someone would say
the city on a hill,
then days would pass in total
silence, unknown bodies
waiting in the dark, that bated
hush along the treeline, where the names
were failing, so it felt like hinterland,
provisional, and never quite
as final as we hoped it might have been,
the way it was in stories: ruin, blossom.

OF GRAMMARYE

In woodcuts,
where the people are asleep

forever, secret
hatcheries of guilt

and curfew
in a Neverland of stars,

I would have made a sorcerer's
apprentice, had I been

less orphaned,
and no history of want

to speak of,
save that glimmer in the woods

where something from the foothills, carcajou
or marten, or a skulk

of foxes blessed with
famine and resolve,

comes stealing through the snow,
in black and white,

to break the spell
I cast against the dark.

A PILGRIM'S PROGRESS

. . . for still as the sinner is awakened about his lost condition,
there ariseth in his soul many fears, and doubts, and discouraging
apprehensions, which all of them get together, and settle
in this place; and this is the reason of the badnesss of this ground.

John Bunyan

How did I end up here, in the furthest
precinct of Despond?
Ziplocked heart, unshriven, one of the many
foragers with evidence enough
to say I was deceived,

I am talking about a devil of some persuasion,
unbiblical, but not without a trace
of sulphur, fire and brimstone being
common in these parts, despite the floods.

Gardens in the mind's eye, unicorns,
a woman and an Angel leaning in
to furnish one another with a God,
but this is all I know of Paradise:
the rest is silence, ruin *à la mode*.

PRAYER

Wer, wenn ich schriee, hörte mich denn aus der Engel Ordnungen?

Rilke

We could cry out now, but no one would ever hear
above the sound of rain against the windows,
trains in the underworld, lit streets filling with traffic.
So let us be skilled in mourning, like the shades
who venture from the earth on days like this,
faces we know amongst the apparitions, voices
calling through the mist, as if they sensed
how close we are to lost, the harvest
squandered, and that cold light on the fields
so unforeseen, before the moon comes up,
it pains us, drained, and distant from a world
we would have set aside, had we been blessed:
the old machinery gone down to dust,
our fathers buried, roofbeams full of stars.

A RECUSANT

If anyone should ask, say I was born
in peacetime, when the roads were bright with frost

and salt was all we knew
of currency.

The old rig in the yard behind the house
more mystery to me than Holy Rood,

the back lanes heaped with snow, a sudden
music in the fence-posts, like the sound

abstention makes
when storyline is done.

I never feed the dogs. They make
their own way, since their gift

is ravening.
But later, when the sky is full of stars,

I go outside,
and know that I am loved.

THE NIGHT FERRY

Had I been less prepared, I would have left
in springtime, when the plum tree in the yard
was still in bloom,
the windows open, after months of snow,
one magpie on the road
and then another.

I could have slipped away, late afternoon,
when everyone was busy somewhere else,
the fish van at the corner, children
dawdling home from school
in twos and threes, a porch light
lit against the dusk on Tolbooth Wynd.

Give me these years again and I will
spend them wisely.
Done with the compass; done, now, with the chart.
The ferry at the dock, lit
stern to bow,
the next life like a footfall in my heart.

ON THE CLICHÉ

Alone at last, I wanted something
lovely to re-use
and care for, hours
of maintenance
and finish, and the sense of *déjà vu*
that comes of being true
to what we know.

Lovely as sleep is lovely to the one
who lies awake till
morning, trying not
to try, until
the otherness bleeds in
and gardens blaze
with something more than light,

the way, in Mediaeval
paintings, when the Angel comes to rest,
the trees, the fruits,
the swallows in the eaves
are brightened from within, and each least thing,
because, and not in spite of what it seems,
is all it is, and all Annunciation.

LOVE STORY

Samarkand never was, though there were
verses in the book that spoke
of lacquerware and lapis lazuli,
the beauty of our goods, delayed for months
at Kandahar or Minsk, the horses
dreaming in the dark behind
their blinkers, nightlong
caravans abroad beneath the sky.

I stood out in the road, by Brewster's Yard,
and waited for a ghost, since ghosts were true,
a pair of Clydesdales pressing to the fence
to listen: rain; the music of the spheres;
or else, those calls I knew, from other lives:
the wind across the sands, a whimbrel's cry.

A FALSE AWAKENING

Only the minor gods have ventured out
this morning:
        delicate
and silken, with a gift for mimicry,
they do not stoop
to punish, or forgive,
though, sometimes, they are capable
of blessing.

I wake at dawn,
   but not to what I know
of Nineveh: a quinquereme
in abstract, certain hues
of cardamon
      or tradescantia;

a siege of herons; razorfish in shoals;
cat-snake and viper
tracked across the floor
or hidden in the feed
at lambing time;

till what I do not recognise
as Silk Road
        or an ounce of *vie en rose,*
is weaselled out of logic by a grace
as final as that fault-line in the mind
where wilderness comes slantwise through the glint
of self-deceit and guile
                to claim its own.

MATINÉE

Mid-afternoon, midsummer; then it
darkens all at once, the traffic

suddenly illumined, daubs
of soft, electric gold

diffusing
in the petrol-coloured rain,

until the town becomes
a cinema: the film about to start,

wings in the backstreets,
limelight on the square,

and all I had omitted in myself
resumed, as if I'd never gone astray.

A POSTSCRIPT, FOR P'ANG YUN

I was thinking about a sainthood.
Drawing water, listening for rain;
or splitting wood at first light in the yard:
the smell of resin, snowmelt in the gravel,
the axe-blade disappearing through the grain.

NOTES & ACKNOWLEDGEMENTS

Bedlam Variations
Largactil (a.k.a. Thorazine) is the trade name for chlorpromazine, once commonly used to treat psychosis.

The Anatomy Lesson of Dr Willem van der Meer
The poem refers to the painting of the same title by Michiel van Miereveld, (born 1 May, 1567, at Delft)

Poem on a Line by Adam Zagajewski
The epigraph here comes from Adam Zagajewski's poem, 'Senior Dance', from the 2014 collection *Asymmetry*, translated by Clare Cavanagh.

In Memoriam
The epigraph is from Adam Zagajewski's poem, 'Nowhere', from *Asymmetry*.

A Postscript, for P'ang Yun
This poem responds to the well-known saying, attributed to the Chinese sage, P'ang Yun: 'How miraculous and wondrous, Hauling water and carrying firewood!'

⋆

Acknowledgements are due to the following publications: *Agenda, London Review of Books, New Humanist, New Statesman*.

The sequence 'Apostasy' was published as a pamphlet by Dare-Gale Press in 2022.